My Catholic Advent and Christmas Activity Book

Reproducible Sheets for Home and School

Written and Illustrated by Jennifer Galvin

Paulist Press

New York/Mahwah, N.J.

For Dad and Mom—who gave me the courage to dream and the tools to succeed

Cover design by Lynn Else
Cover illustration by Jennifer Galvin

Text and illustrations copyright © 2004 by Jennifer Galvin

The scripture quotations contained herein are from, or adapted from, the New Revised Standard Version Bible, copyright © 1989 by the Division of Christian Education of the National Council of the Churches of Christ in the U.S.A., and are used by permission. All rights reserved.

ISBN: 0-8091-6720-4

Published by Paulist Press
997 Macarthur Boulevard
Mahwah, New Jersey 07430

www.paulistpress.com

Printed and bound in the United States of America.

The New Liturgical Year

Catholics celebrate a year that is based on the events of Christ's life.

Across

3. Catholics live in _ _ _ _ _ _ time
   by following the events of Christ's life.
4. During Advent we remember how long people had to wait for _ _ _ _ _.
6. The _ _ _ _ _ _ _ _ _ _ or church year begins with Advent.
7. On _ _ _ _ _ _ _ _ _ we celebrate Jesus' birth.
10. Celebrating the year around sacred time reminds us there is another _ _ _ _ beyond this life.
11. Only by living in sacred time do we start to understand how much God loves us and how to live in his _ _ _ _ more deeply and truly.

Down

1. _ _ _ _ _ _ _ _ _ _ celebrate a year that is based on the events of Christ's life.
2. _ _ _ _ _ _ _ begins a new liturgical year.
5. During the Christmas season we remember Jesus' life from when he was born to when he was _ _ _ _ _ _ _ _ _ and began his ministry.
8. There is the _ _ _ _ of this world, and also sacred time that happens at the same moment.
9. A _ _ _ _ in the outside world begins January 1 and ends December 31.

Countdown to Christmas

Write in the dates of the month in the candles. Then cut out the special days of Advent and glue them onto your Advent calendar.

December

Sunday	Monday	Tuesday	Wednesday	Thursday	Friday	Saturday

First Sunday of Advent

Second Sunday of Advent

Third Sunday of Advent

Fourth Sunday of Advent

Christmas Vigil

Christmas Day!

Advent Prayer Word Find

Traditionally we pray this prayer every night during Advent until Christmas Eve. Find all of the words in the prayer that are in **bold** print.

```
H A B P R A M E R I T S X D X Z H
L O V L H N P R A H P R A Y E R Z
H H O P E X B E Y H P H B L H O X
O M B M R S X V O U C H S A F E H
L M A R B W S Z V O H X B E T H M
Y M I D N U X E R P D E M G L H I
M O Z P S R G H D B H E V V P H D
O M M E B E N H R L H L R V U P N
T E J T R O M N X E G H C V R L I
H N C I S B C H L X R S T I E B G
E T R T P C G H V C N P B R C C H
R C X I J K T P M T N A R G R R T
Z B D O X E V O L S D C L I X N P
B R J N B I J P I E R C I N G V H
J L G S J O L C X L B D C J T R D
G R C D S B R B H T I A F V V O X
L I A H C L B N X R S T M N G R T
```

Hail and **blessed** be the hour and the **moment** when the **Son** of **God** was **born** of the most **pure Virgin** in **Bethlehem** at **midnight** in the **piercing** cold. In that hour **vouchsafe**, O my God, to hear my **prayer** and **grant** my **petitions** through the **merits** of **Jesus** Christ and His most **holy mother**. **Amen**.

Bonus—Can you find the words **faith, love,** and **hope**?

Lighting the Advent Wreath

The Advent wreath is lit one candle at a time on the four Sundays before Christmas. An Advent wreath has three purple candles and one pink candle. The pink candle is lit on the third Sunday. Color the Advent wreaths and match each wreath with the Sunday of Advent it represents.

Candle of Joy
(Third Sunday of Advent)

Candle of Love
(Fourth Sunday of Advent)

Candle of Peace
(Second Sunday of Advent)

Candle of Hope
(First Sunday of Advent)

Copyright © 2004, *My Catholic Advent and Christmas Activity Book*. Published by Paulist Press.

The Unexpected Hour

No one knows when the Son of Man will return. We must keep our hearts pure and our souls ready as we await his return. Do the subtraction problems. Then fill in the blanks at the bottom with the letter that matches each answer. Then read what we do while we wait for Jesus to return.

A:___=6-1   H:___=7-4   O:___=9-3   V :___=23-2

B:___=26-0   I :___=20-1   P:___=12-2   W:___=10-3

C:___=9-7   J :___=19-2   Q:___=17-4   X :___=19-4

D:___=8-4   K:___=14-3   R:___=24-2   Y :___=10-2

E:___=26-3   L :___=26-2   S:___=24-4   Z :___=26-1

F:___=10-1   M:___=15-3   T:___=19-3

G:___=16-2   N:___=19-1   U:___=1-0

___ ___ ___ ___ ___   ___ ___ ___   ___ ___ ___ ___
7   5   16   2   3   5   18   4   10   22   5   8

The Immaculate Conception

We believe Mary was born without sin. That is why God asked her to be the mother of Jesus. What did Mary say when God sent the angel Gabriel to ask her to be Jesus' mother? Follow the line from each heart to a box, and put the letter from that heart in the box.

Luke 1:38

Luke 1:38

John the Baptist

John the Baptist baptized people with water and told people that Jesus was coming to baptize them with the Holy Spirit. Color John and the people waiting to be baptized. Baptism is one of the seven sacraments.

The Messenger

A messenger preached by the river Jordan and baptized people in the river. He told people Jesus would come after him and baptize them with the Holy Spirit. What was that man's name?

To find the answer, look at the symbols under each space below. Use the chart to find which letter goes in each space. Follow the first symbol across and the second symbol up to find each letter. Put the letter in the space.

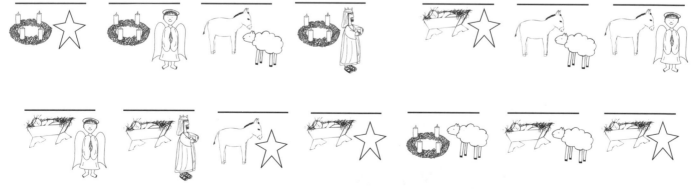

A Special Visitor

When God decided to send his only Son to this Earth, he sent a special message to Mary, and later, a special message to Joseph. Color by number to find out who brought God's messages to Earth.

1=Yellow 2=Purple 3=White 4=Your skin color 5=Blue

Mary Visits Elizabeth

Do the subtraction problems. Then fill in the blanks
at the bottom with the letter that matches each answer.

A: ___ =7-5   H: ___ =26-3   O: ___ =7-2   V: ___ =24-2
B: ___ =9-2   I: ___ =18-2   P: ___ =19-2   W: ___ =15-1
C: ___ =24-0   J: ___ =16-1   Q: ___ =21-1   X: ___ =16-3
D: ___ =10-2   K: ___ =23-2   R: ___ =14-3   Y: ___ =20-1
E: ___ =1-0   L: ___ =10-1   S: ___ =6-3   Z: ___ =29-3
F: ___ =14-4   M: ___ =7-3   T: ___ =19-1
G: ___ =9-3   N: ___ =26-1   U: ___ =14-2

Mary went to visit her cousin Elizabeth, the mother of John the Baptist. Elizabeth was filled with the Holy Spirit when Mary greeted her. Fill in the blanks to find out part of what Elizabeth said to Mary. If you want to know more, read Luke 1:39–45.

"
___ ___ ___ ___ ___ ___ ___   ___ ___ ___   ___ ___ ___
7   9   1   3   3   1   8   2   11 1   19 5   12

___ ___ ___ ___ ___   ___ ___ ___ ___ ___,   ___ ___ ___
2   4   5   25 6   14 5   4   1   25   2   25 8

___ ___ ___ ___ ___ ___ ___   ___ ___   ___ ___ ___
7   9   1   3   3   1   8   16 3   18 23 1

                                                    "
___ ___ ___ ___ ___   ___ ___   ___ ___ ___ ___   ___ ___ ___ ___.
10 11 12 16 18   5   10   19 5   12 11   14 5   4   7

Luke 1:42

Fourth Sunday of Advent: C
12

An Angel Appears to Joseph

An angel appeared to Joseph in a dream and said, "Joseph, son of David, do not be afraid to take Mary as your wife, for the child in her is from the Holy Spirit. She will bear a son, and you are to name him Jesus, for he will save his people from their sins." Adapted from Matthew 1:20–21

Find all fifteen things that are different in the second picture.

Mary and Joseph Travel to Bethlehem

When Caesar Augustus decreed that everyone must go to their own town to be counted, Joseph and Mary traveled to Bethlehem to register. Help Mary and Joseph travel through the maze to Bethlehem.

The Shepherds Visit Jesus

"When the angels had left them and gone into heaven, the shepherds said to one another, 'Let us go now to Bethlehem and see this thing that has taken place, which the Lord has made known to us.'" Luke 2:15

Find all sixteen things that are different in the second picture.

The Word

"In the beginning was the Word, and the Word was with God, and the Word was God." John 1:1

The Book of John begins with the above sentence. John calls Jesus "the Word." This is a hard idea to understand and has puzzled many people. A note in the Bible says, "The Word of God is more than speech; it is God in action and Jesus is this 'Word.'" In the rest of the Book of John, Jesus is described in other ways that are easier to understand because they come from everyday life. Below are some of the words John uses to describe Jesus in the rest of his book. Match each word to where it appears in the Gospel of John. Then look it up and read about it. The pictures are clues to help you match.

1. Teacher

A. John 6:35

2. The Vine

B. John 12:24

3. Bread of Life

C. John 10:11

4. Grain of Wheat

D. John 4:10

5. Gift of God

E. John 4:10

6. The Gate

F. John 8:12

7. The Good Shepherd

G. John 3:2

8. King of Israel

H. John 15:5

9. Lamb of God

I. John 1:49

10. Light of the World

J. John 10:9

11. (Well of) Living Water

K. John 1:29

A Bed for Baby Jesus

There was no room at the inn in Bethlehem for Mary and Joseph to stay. So Jesus was born in a stable. Connect the dots to find out what Mary used as a bed for the baby Jesus. Then color the picture and unscramble the word to answer the question below it.

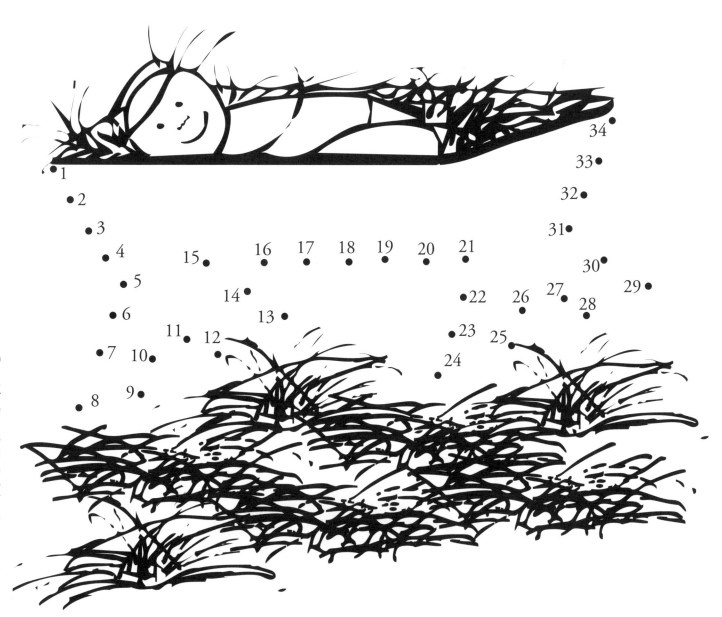

Mary put baby Jesus in a _ _ _ _ _ _. AEGRMN

The Christmas Crèche

St. Francis of Assisi created a live version of the nativity scene in a cave with a manger and live animals. This is called a crèche. The crèche helps us remember that God loved us so much he sent his son to live among us. The crèche also helps us remember that Jesus came not as a king, but as one of the poor and humble. We can join with the poor by trying to be as humble as Jesus and by denying ourselves things we really don't need.

Unscramble these words to find out some of the lessons of the crèche.

1. _ _ _ _ _ _ _ _ IILYUMTH is one of the lessons of the crèche.

2. Another lesson of the crèche is _ _ _ _ _ _ _ TVYOEPR of spirit.

3. St. Francis also wanted people to learn _ _ _ _ LFSE-_ _ _ _ _ _ LNEAID as a lesson from the Christmas crèche.

4. _ _ _ _ _ _ _ GIIOJNN with the _ _ _ _ OORP is a fourth lesson that we can learn from the Christmas crèche.

5. God's _ _ _ _ _ GATRE _ _ _ _ VEOL for us in the _ _ _ _ _ _ _ _ _ _ _ NNCRNAAIITO is another one of the lessons of the crèche that St Francis would have liked people to learn.

An Angel Appears

"Then an angel of the Lord stood before them and the glory of the Lord shone around them and they were terrified. But the angel said to them, 'Do not be afraid; for see—I am bringing you good news of great joy for all the people: to you is born this day in the city of David a Savior, who is the Messiah, the Lord.'" Luke 2:9–11

Find and circle all twenty-two things that are wrong with this picture.

The Shepherds Visit Bethlehem

Help the shepherds get to Bethlehem to visit Jesus and then back to watch their sheep.

Nativity Word Find

Here is the story of Jesus' birth as told in Luke. Find the words in the passage that are in **bold** print.

```
F I R F I F I R S T B O R N R N B
J J J F B J R F S T S O J R N J N
T I M E T T R F E R S S R N R O X
C T F R S B W W B N R O F V H S H
C T H R B U W V R C G B N V C E V
H R H B H J S H J A N A J F R P S
I H D E L I V E R H P V G J B H J
L C W J E M V R M J D P H E V B E
D X M B S X R J B E R V E R D R S
W C A D B N P V R B Y J W D F H B
B T N M J K B E N A T I V I T Y R
A A G G V T T B C C T M W R C Y W
B V E B T S V P L T C M I R C W Y
L W R J I B V L J V I B R V L W S
R Y V G S R W A V X W N T M O S T
M N E J V M B C T F B M G R T W A
B R J N N I V E B J M A R Y H B R
```

Joseph went to Bethlehem to be **registered** with **Mary**, to whom he was **engaged** and who was **expecting** a **child**. While they were there, the **time** came to **deliver** her child. She gave **birth** to her **firstborn son** and **wrapped** him in **bands** of **cloth**, and laid him in a **manger**, because there was no **place** for them in the **inn**. Luke 2:5–7 (adapted)

Bonus—Can you find the words **Jesus**, **star**, and **nativity**?

Christmas Day

Color by number to find out who was born on Christmas Day.

1=White 2=Purple 3=Yellow 4=Gray 5=Dark Blue
6=Brown 7=Green 8=Light Brown 9=Your skin color

Feast of St. Stephen

Read or listen to the story of St. Stephen in Acts 6:2–6, 8–10; 7:54–60. Then match the word or phrase on the left with the correct definition on the right.

December 26

"Look," he said, "I see the heavens opened and the Son of Man standing at the right hand of God." Acts 7:56

Deacon

The Feast of St. Stephen is sometimes also called this. It is celebrated by giving boxes of money to the less fortunate.

Martyr

What Stephen was doing among the people.

Stones

The job that St. Stephen was appointed to do for the church.

Prayed

What St. Stephen did while the crowd was stoning him.

Boxing Day

Someone who dies for his or her beliefs.

St. Stephen's vision

The day the feast of St. Stephen is celebrated.

Wonders and signs

What the crowd used to kill St. Stephen.

Mary, Joseph, and Jesus Escape to Egypt

After the wise men came and visited Jesus, Joseph was warned by an angel in a dream that he should take Mary and Jesus and flee to Egypt, for they were not safe in Bethlehem. And they got up and fled in the night. We celebrate this day as the feast of the Holy Innocents. Find and circle all fifteen things that are wrong with this picture. Then color the picture.

Feast of the Holy Family

The feast of the Holy Family is celebrated to remind us to be content with and thankful for everyday life. We remember that Mary, Joseph, and Jesus were an ideal family, and we try to live as they lived. This crossword is based, in part, on Col 3:12–21. In this letter, Paul was reminding the church how to act like good followers of Jesus.

Across

2. We should let the peace of Christ rule in our _ _ _ _ _ _.
3. We should be _ _ _ _ _ _ _ and happy with our lives.
6. We should _ _ _ _ _ _ _ _ each other, just as the Lord has forgiven us.
8. Above all, we should _ _ _ _ each other, for love binds us together in harmony.
9. Some people think that everyday life is _ _ _ _ and boring. We should see life as a precious gift.

Down

1. We should be _ _ _ _ _ _ _ _ _ for our everyday lives.
4. Mary, Joseph, and Jesus are the _ _ _ _ _ family.
5. We should show _ _ _ _ _ _ _ _ _ and compassion to one another.
7. Children today should _ _ _ _ their parents just as Jesus obeyed his parents.

The Solemnity of Mary

Crack the code to find the answer to the question below. Do the addition problems. Then fill in the blanks with the letter that matches the number under the blank.

A:___=1+0   H:___=7+5   O:___=5+6   V:___=10+8

B:___=12+12   I:___=3+1   P:___=10+9   W:___=20+3

C:___=2+3   J:___=7+6   Q:___=15+10   X:___=9+11

D:___=5+1   K:___=13+13   R:___=5+3   Y:___=9+8

E:___=1+1   L:___=9+6   S:___=5+2   Z:___=20+1

F:___=7+7   M:___=3+6   T:___=11+11

G:___=4+6   N:___=8+8   U:___=3+0

When the shepherds went to Bethlehem to see Jesus, they told everyone about the angels that had appeared to them in the fields to tell them about Jesus' birth. People who heard the shepherds' story were amazed. Mary had a different response. Fill in the blanks to see what Mary did.

"

___ ___ ___   ___ ___ ___ ___   ___ ___ ___ ___ ___ ___ ___ ___ ___
24 3 22   9 1 8 17   22 8 2 1 7 3 8 2 6

___ ___ ___   ___ ___ ___ ___ ___   ___ ___ ___ ___ ___
1 15 15   22 12 2 7 2   23 11 8 6 7

___ ___ ___   ___ ___ ___ ___ ___ ___ ___   ___ ___ ___ ___
1 16 6   19 11 16 6 2 8 2 6   22 12 2 9

___ ___ ___ ___ ___   ___ ___ ___ ___ ___ ___ ." Luke 2:19
4 16 12 2 8   12 2 1 8 22

A Sign in the Sky

Color the picture, then answer the question below.

1=Blue 2=Purple 3=Green 4=Yellow

What appeared in the sky to guide the wise men to Jesus?_____

Epiphany
27

Epiphany

On Epiphany, January 6, we celebrate the day the three kings came to visit Jesus. Help these three kings bring their gifts to baby Jesus.

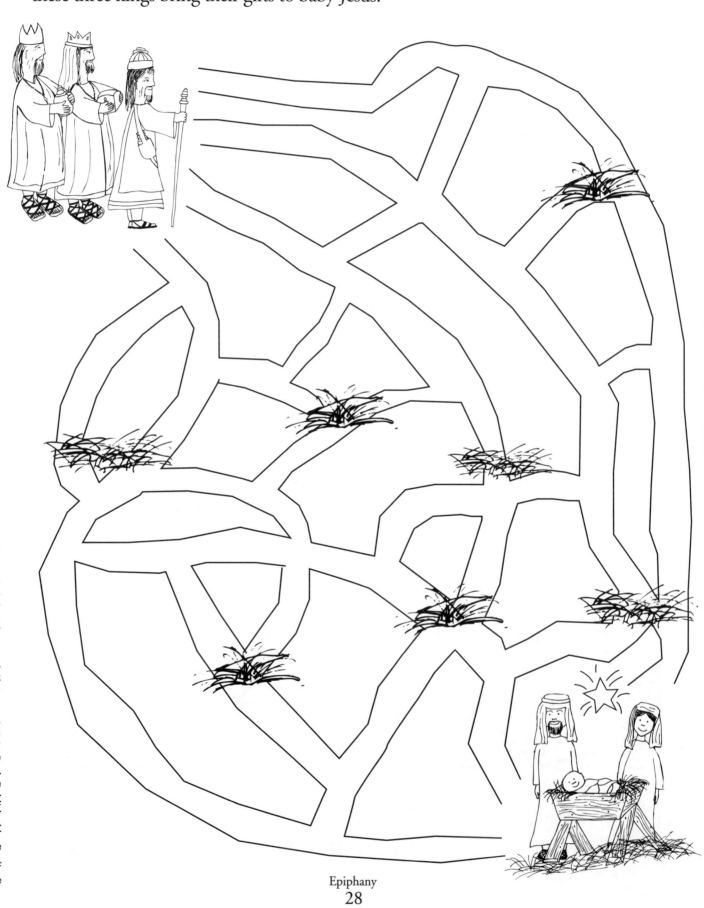

The Three Kings

Traditionally, we believe that there were three kings, or wise men, who visited Jesus. First, find and circle the three kings who are exactly the same. Then unscramble the names of the gifts the three wise men brought to Jesus.

What were the gifts that the three wise men brought to baby Jesus?
_ _ _ _ OLDG _ _ _ _ _ _ _ _ _ _ _ AINCEEFKNSNR and _ _ _ _ _ HYMRR.

Baptism of Our Lord

The day that Jesus was baptized was a very special day. This was the day he chose to publicly dedicate his life to serving God, his heavenly Father. As we celebrate the baptism of Jesus, we also remember the importance of our own baptism and our own dedication to the Lord. We celebrate Jesus' baptism the Sunday after Epiphany. Unscramble the words and fill in the blanks to find out more.

1. Jesus was baptized in the _ _ _ _ _ _ River. AORJDN

2. _ _ _ _ NJHO the _ _ _ _ _ _ _ STTAIPB baptized Jesus.

3. John the Baptist baptized people with _ _ _ _ _. EATRW

4. John proclaimed that Jesus would baptize people with the _ _ _ _ OYLH _ _ _ _ _ _. IIPRTS

5. After Jesus was baptized, the _ _ _ _ _ _ _ opened. EAHVNES

6. God sent the Holy Spirit to Jesus after his baptism in the form of a _ _ _ _. EOVD

7. God told us that Jesus is his beloved _ _ _. NSO

8. When Jesus was baptized, God also said that he was well _ _ _ _ _ _ _ PSLEDEA with Jesus.

Baptism of Jesus

30

Answers

Page 8

"HERE AM I THE SERVANT OF THE LORD." Luke 1:38

Page 3

```
        ¹C              ²A
  ³S A C R E D          D
        T         ⁴J E S U S
        H         E
        O         ⁵B
  ⁶L I T U R G I C A L
        I         P
  ⁷C H R I S T M A S    T   ⁹Y
        S     ⁸T        ¹⁰L I F E
              I         Z   A
              M         E   R
              ¹¹L O V E D
              E
```

Page 6

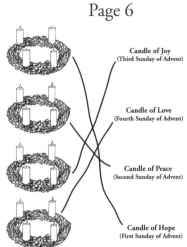

Candle of Joy (Third Sunday of Advent)

Candle of Love (Fourth Sunday of Advent)

Candle of Peace (Second Sunday of Advent)

Candle of Hope (First Sunday of Advent)

Page 7

A: 5 =6-1   H: 3 =7-4   O: 6 =9-3   V:21=23-2
B:26=26-0   I:19=20-1   P:10=12-2   W: 7 =10-3
C: 2 =9-7   J:17=19-2   Q:13=17-4   X:15=19-4
D: 4 =8-4   K:11=14-3   R:22=24-2   Y: 8 =10-2
E:23=26-3   L:24=26-2   S:20=24-4   Z:25=26-1
F: 9 =10-1   M:12=15-3   T:16=19-3
G:14=16-2   N:18=19-1   U: 1 =1-0

W A T C H   A N D   P R A Y
7 5 16 2 3   5 18 4   10 22 5 8

Page 13

Page 14

Page 10

JOHN THE BAPTIST

Page 18

1. HUMILITY is one of the lessons of the crèche.

2. Another lesson of the crèche is POVERTY of spirit.

3. St. Francis also wanted people to learn SELF-DENIAL as a lesson from the Christmas crèche.

4. JOINING with the POOR is a fourth lesson that we can learn from the Christmas crèche.

5. God's GREAT LOVE for us in the INCARNATION is another one of the lessons of the crèche that St Francis would have liked people to learn.

Page 12

A: 2 =7-5   H:23=26-3   O: 5 =7-2   V:22 =24-2
B: 7 =9-2   I: 16=18-2   P:17=19-2   W:14=15-1
C:24=24-0   J: 15=16-1   Q:20=21-1   X:13 =16-3
D: 8 =10-2   K:21=23-2   R:11=14-3   Y:19 =20-1
E: 1 =1-0   L: 9 =10-1   S: 3 =6-3   Z:26 =29-3
F:10=14-4   M: 4 =7-3   T:18=19-1
G: 6 =9-3   N:25=26-1   U:12=14-2

"B L E S S E D   A R E   Y O U
 7 9 1 3 3 1 8   2 11 1   19 5 12

A M O N G   W O M E N   A N D
2 4 5 25 6   14 5 4 1 25'   2 25 8

B L E S S E D   I S   T H E
7 9 1 3 3 1 8   1 3   1 18 1

F R U I T   O F   Y O U R   W O M B"
10 11 12 16 18   5 10   19 5 12 11   14 5 4 7'

Page 17

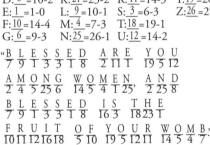

Mary put baby Jesus in a MANGER.

Page 5

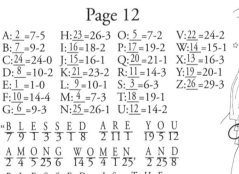

Page 19

Page 15

Answers

Page 20

Page 16

1. Teacher — G. John 3:2
2. The Vine — H. John 15:5
3. Bread of Life — A. John 6:35
4. Grain of Wheat — B. John 12:24
5. Gift of God — D. John 4:10
6. The Gate — J. John 10:9
7. The Good Shepherd — C. John 10:11
8. King of Israel — I. John 1:49
9. Lamb of God — K. John 1:29
10. Light of the World — F. John 8:12
11. (Well of) Living Water — E. John 4:10

Page 21

Word search grid containing: FIRSTBORN, TIME, DELIVER, NATIVITY, STAR, MARY, and other circled words.

Page 24

Coloring/find-the-objects picture of the Nativity scene.

Page 23

December 26	"Look," he said, "I see the heavens opened and the Son of Man standing at the right hand of God." Acts 7:56
Deacon	The Feast of St. Stephen is sometimes also called this. It is celebrated by giving boxes of money to the less fortunate.
Martyr	What Stephen was doing among the people.
Stones	The job that St. Stephen was appointed to for the church.
Prayed	What St. Stephen did while the crowd was stoning him.
Boxing Day	Someone who dies for his or her beliefs.
St. Stephen's vision	The day the feast of St. Stephen is celebrated.
Wonders and Signs	What the crowd used to kill St. Stephen.

Page 25

Crossword answers:
2. HEARTS
3. CONTENT
6. FORGIVE
8. LOVE
9. DULL

Down answers: THANKFUL, CONTENT, IDEA, KINDNESS, FORBY, DARKNESS

Page 26

A: 1 =1+0   H:12=7+5   O:11=5+6   V:18=10+8
B:24=12+12   I: 4 =3+1   P:19=10+9   W:23=20+3
C: 5 =2+3   J:13=7+6   Q:25=15+10 X:20=9+11
D: 6 =5+1   K:26=13+13   R: 8 =5+3   Y:17=9+8
E: 2 =1+1   L:15=9+6   S: 7 =5+2   Z:21=20+1
F:14=7+7   M: 9 =3+6   T:22=11+11
G:10=4+6   N:16=8+8   U: 3 =3+0

"BUT MARY TREASURED
 24 3 22 9 1 8 17 22 8 2 1 7 3 8 2 6

ALL THESE WORDS
1 15 15 22 12 2 7 2 23 11 8 6 7

AND PONDERED THEM
1 16 6 19 11 16 6 2 8 2 6 22 12 2 9

IN HER HEART." Luke 2:19
4 16 12 2 8 12 2 1 8 22

Page 28

Maze picture.

Page 29

What were the gifts that the three wise men brought to baby Jesus?
GOLD, FRANKINCENSE, AND MYRRH.

Page 27

What appeared in the sky to guide the wise men to Jesus? A STAR

Page 30

1. Jesus was baptized in the JORDAN River.
2. JOHN the BAPTIST baptized Jesus.
3. John the Baptist baptized people with WATER.
4. John proclaimed Jesus would baptize people with the HOLY SPIRIT.
5. After Jesus was baptized, the HEAVENS opened.
6. God sent the Holy Spirit to Jesus after his baptism in the form of a DOVE.
7. God told us that Jesus is his beloved SON.
8. When Jesus was baptized, God also said that he was well PLEASED with Jesus.